School and Society in England

in England

*Social Backgrounds of Oxford
and Cambridge Students*

By C. Arnold Anderson and Miriam Schnaper
UNIVERSITY OF KENTUCKY

GREENWOOD PRESS, PUBLISHERS
WESTPORT, CONNECTICUT

The Library of Congress has catalogued this publication as follows:

Library of Congress Cataloging in Publication Data

Anderson, Charles Arnold, 1907–
    School and society in England.

        Original ed. issued in series: Annals of American
    research.
        1. Oxford. University--Students. 2. Cambridge.
    University--Students. I. Schnaper, Miriam, joint
    author. II. Title. III. Series: Annals of
    American research.
    ⌈LF529.A55 1972⌉   378.1'98'0942   70-138142
    ISBN 0-8371-5599-1

Originally published in 1952
by Public Affairs Press, Washington, D.C.

Reprinted with the permission
of Public Affairs Press

First Greenwood Reprinting 1972

Library of Congress Catalogue Card Number 70-138142

ISBN 0-8371-5599-1

Printed in the United States of America

SCHOOL AND SOCIETY IN ENGLAND

SOCIAL BACKGROUNDS OF OXFORD AND CAMBRIDGE STUDENTS

By C. Arnold Anderson and Miriam Schnaper

For seven centuries the great universities of Oxford and Cambridge stood alone as leaders of higher education in England. It was not until well into the nineteenth century that other colleges arose to occupy a growing place. Who attended these universities over this period from the middle ages to the maturity of capitalism? And what positions did these graduates of Oxford and Cambridge occupy in English society? For the first centuries we have only indirect clues. One brief summary of the social backgrounds of Oxford students at the end of the seventeenth century has been published, and there is a report on one Cambridge class in the 1930's. For that period in which England emerged as an industrial nation no data have heretofore been available. It was during this period that the entire structure of English life changed and that attitudes shifted from "each man in his proper place" toward a more democratic point of view.

The primary purpose of the present study is to fill the gap by presenting an analysis of the students matriculating at the two universities for the period from 1752 to 1886, the period for which alumni directories of both schools have been published. The information on the recent Cambridge graduates will then be re-examined in the light of the older record. A brief supplementary examination of the educational backgrounds of persons listed in *Who's Who* and the *Dictionary of National Biography* will enable us to point up the roles of other universities and of universities generally in training the outstanding men of England. The samples and methods used are described in the appendix. Before presenting these analyses, however, it will be helpful to review the historical background.

The First Five Centuries

When the foundations of Oxford and Cambridge were laid the only bodies able to support education were the throne, the great landlords, and the Church. A few of the wealthier landed nobility participated in the revival of learning and aided some of their retainers to do so, but the principal scholars of those early days were

---

* The authors appreciate the critical assistance of Dr. Carl Cone, Professor of English History at the University of Kentucky. They ask the patience of British readers with their efforts to thread the labyrinth of English custom, social and educational.

1

ecclesiastics. Albert Mansbridge appears to be in agreement with
other historians in stressing the large proportion of poor among these
early students: "The Church depended for its very existence on a
regular supply of skilled 'clerks'. There is little need to stress the
obvious truth that the great statesmen and ecclesiastics of medieval
England were as a rule men who had been born in humble circumstances." [1]

Though this judgment may be an exaggeration, it appears legitimate
to conclude that at this early date the secular nobility and gentry
were of much less relative importance in the student body than later.
The students at the then new universities would formerly have been
educated in the monastic and cathedral schools. Most of them were
mature men already established in vocations even though in modest
worldly circumstances. This situation persisted after the establish-
ment of the colleges in the fourteenth and fifteenth centuries, for,
as Mansbridge says (p. 108), "the early Colleges were devised for
poor scholars, not because they were poor, but because they were
scholars. . . . The Statutes of the Colleges were studded with poverty clauses."

Gradually, however, well-to-do sons of the gentry became more
numerous in the student body. This new trend was facilitated by the
dissolution of the monasteries and the suppression of religious orders.[2]
Along with the scholars admitted under poverty clauses, an increasing
number of paying guests were admitted as Commoners and Pensioners.
This development was well advanced by the end of the sixteenth
century, though sons of "plebeian" fathers still constituted a sizeable
plurality. A parallel change occurred in the grammar schools.

The status of the fathers of Oxford entrants for the years 1572-1621
has been reported by Andrew Clark.[3] Several interesting shifts took
place during this half century. Plebeians accounted for 60 percent of
the matriculants as the last quarter of the 16th century began, but
their proportion dropped steadily to 40 percnt in 1602-11, recovering
to 45 percent in the next decade. They were the only group to decline
(slightly) in actual numbers over the period. Meanwhile the representation of sons of clergymen rose steadily, until from only 1.2 percent at first they came to make up 12.6 percent in 1612-21. Sons of
esquires and country gentlemen climbed from a third to 47 percent
at the end of the sixteenth century and dropped back again to a third
two decades later. In brief, over this half-century the gentry gained
and then lost again, the clergy forged ahead, and the plebeians lost
ground. (Sons of knights rose from 3 to 7 percent of the matriculants.)

Something over a century later, to anticipate, these changes had proceeded much further. By the mid-eighteenth century only an eighth of the Oxford entrants were plebeians, a fourth were sons of military officers and another fourth sons of gentry or esquires, and nearly a third came from rectories. Even if the military here are taken as comparable to many of the earlier plebeians, the transformation is marked. Most of those labeled "military" in the later data were from families of the secular nobility, knights, esquires, and country gentlemen, indicating that this group had gained appreciably among the students.

Students at Oxford and Cambridge, 1752-1886

During the period covered by our study, several new universities arose in Britain. While Oxford and Cambridge stood substantially alone at the start they were no longer the whole of higher education at the end of the nineteenth century. The bias in student recruitment was probably a consistent one, several influences making for narrower selection at Oxford and Cambridge than elsewhere.

In 1750 both universities were steeped in "the classical tradition", which was indeed vocational training for the church and other learned occupations. Oxford leaned even more heavily upon the classics than did Cambridge. When the need for new professions became evident, these universities had neither desire nor equipment to meet the demand. The later creation of the University of London as well as the provincial universities was in part a reflection of this discrepancy between need and curriculum at the traditional schools. Moreover the University of Edinburgh and the Royal College of Physicians and Surgeons drew many potential Oxford and Cambridge students while the Inns of Court, although independent of universities, prepared men for the bar. Of considerable, although as yet unmeasured, importance was the fact that until 1858 at Cambridge and later at Oxford students who were non-conformists could not take degrees; they could not enter Oxford and were admitted only under special circumstances at Cambridge. These restrictions, combined with the luxury character of the students' lives, undoubtedly narrowed the groups from which students were drawn. Social selection was further intensified by the association between vocation and denomination that accompanied the separation of the newer churches.

Internal Stratification and Scholarships

The internal student hierarchy of the universities reflected on the one hand the aristocratic social structure of England and, on the

other, the heritage of provisions for educating the capable children of
the less privileged families. It has been estimated that in 1800 there
were about 750 Oxford and 400 Cambridge students. Of these, about
a sixth were "Noblemen" (Cambridge) and "Gentlemen Commoners"
(Oxford) who lived luxuriously with their servants, enjoyed special
privileges, and dined with the college heads. About a half were
"Commoners" (Oxford) and "Fellow Commoners" and "Pensioners"
(Cambridge)—men who could well afford the university but not the
extreme luxury of the first group. The remaining students were about
equal parts "Servitors" (Oxford) or "Sizars" (Cambridge) and "Foun-
dation Scholars"; these students performed menial duties, often as
servants of the nobles and Gentlemen Commoners.[4]

Who were these scholars, servitors, and sizars? Of the "scholars"
between 1750 and 1850, Mansbridge writes, "They had to swear poverty, but like other oaths required at the universities this was regarded
as a matter of form. These Scholars usually became Fellows after-
wards, and again found it easy to conform to custom and take the
necessary oaths."

Nevertheless, the "close scholarships" (confined to particular pre-
paratory schools, districts, or family connections) enabled some students of relatively moderate means to be educated at Oxford or
Cambridge and especially at the latter. That Cambridge attracted
more such scholars reflected also its earlier cultivation of mathematics
—Cambridge setting up the Mathematical Tripos in 1747, fifty years
ahead of Oxford.

The Oxford Servitors were in a far more menial position than the
Sizars at Cambridge. The former remained unemancipated to the
time they were abolished, in 1854; they were clothed distinctively and
restricted by sharply stratified codes of behavior. On the other hand,
despite the contempt of the Cambridge fellow commoner for the poor
man, the Sizars gradually won an increasingly respected position.

"There is, in point of fact, an obvious difference between the term
'Servitor' as compared with 'Sizar'. The latter is merely one who drew
a 'size' or a portion of bread or drink and its Oxford equivalent would
be a Battler. To size at Cambridge, or to battle at Oxford, was to
set down in the Buttery Book the quantum of food taken.

"With this we can end our account of the Cambridge Sizar, who,
gradually establishing his equality with the Pensioner, and finding
himself confused not once, or twice, with the Scholars, passed on to
the heights of academic dignity and power. Superior he usually was
in learning and intelligence to all the gilt-arrayed noblemen who
passed through on their way but are forgotten . . ."

The reforms of the two universities in the middle of the nineteenth century had mixed effects. Abolition of the system by which poor students acted as servants and doing away with distinctive dress and special privileges for the nobility and the most wealthy were expressions of democratic ideas (or, at least, bourgeois ideas) within the universities. On the other hand these changes no doubt diminished the opportunities for poor boys. At the same time the "poverty clauses" which had survived the centuries were abolished in the interest of a system of "merit". The reduction in number of "close scholarships" theoretically made for greater equality of opportunity to secure scholarships. This policy was designed to raise the level of performance, but it may in practice have worked against the poor student who could not afford the costly preparation at the "Public" schools. The problem was aggravated by the persisting requirement of Greek for entrance while its teaching was being given up in the grammar schools in line with the policies of the Charity Commissioners. Only the more brilliant partially self-taught student of a humbler school might hope to succeed in competition with the graduates of more expensive schools. These handicaps for students from families of modest incomes were neutralized gradually by the increase in scholarships in universities and in lower schools. Nevertheless, during the last half of the nineteenth century it was exceedingly difficult for a poor boy to enter Oxford or Cambridge.

Social Backgrounds

Against the background already sketched, it is not surprising to find (Table 1) that between 1752 and 1886 three social strata stood out as of primary (and of about equal) importance in supplying students to Oxford and Cambridge: gentry, clergy, and military. Together they accounted for four-fifths of all students. No other set of fathers contributed a large share of matriculants, although it is evident that the nobility and to a lesser extent law and medicine are represented in numbers far above their proportion of national population.[5]

The gentry and nobility are not so sharply differentiated from the military and clergy as the designations in these tables might suggest. The younger sons of nobles often became officers; nobles who had active military careers were given the latter designation. Also, younger sons of the gentry often entered the armed forces and the clergy; thus many of the students who were sons of military and clergy fathers were grandsons of gentry. "Plebeians" ranged from business employees, government employees (outside the topmost

1: SOCIAL STATUS OF MATRICULANTS AND THEIR FATHERS: OXFORD AND CAMBRIDGE UNIVERSITIES, 1752-1886

Status Categories	Distribution of Fathers			Distribution of Students		
	OXFORD	CAMBRIDGE(a)	BOTH(a)	OXFORD	CAMBRIDGE(a)	BOTH(a)
Nobility	3.6%	7.2%	5.1%	7.0%	4.7%	5.5%
Gentry	28.1	25.5	27.1	7.5	5.8	6.4
Clergy	23.3	32.6	27.0	64.2	54.3	58.0
Military	39.0	6.0	25.5	2.4	4.5	3.7
Law	.6	5.3	2.5	8.7	11.2	10.3
Medicine	2.5	6.0	4.0	.7	3.5	2.5
Government	°	1.5	.6	2.4	1.6	1.9
Business	.1	9.4	3.9	.6	3.9	2.7
Academic	—	3.3	1.4	5.4	9.1	7.7
Plebeian	2.7	3.2	2.9	1.1	1.4	1.3
	100.0	100.0	100.0	100.0	100.0	100.0
Total	2,566	1,769	4,335	1,272	2,247	3,519
Not Given	10	1,053	1,063	1,304	575	1,879
Grand Total	2,576	2,822	5,398	2,576	2,822	5,398

(a) Adding the probable totals of Cambridge names beginning K to Z to those of the sample for letters A to J; see Appendix.
° Not over .05 percent.

ranks who were put under government), through yeomanry, husband-men, writers and artists, and miscellaneous occupations. Not all coming from plebeian homes were necessarily from "poor" homes; the latter were probably exceptions, especially in the latter part of the period.

The students of the two universities came from strikingly different sectors of society. Thus the military constituted 39 percent of the Oxford fathers but only 6 percent of Cambridge fathers. Sons of clergymen were more numerous at Cambridge. In total, Cambridge drew its students from a much wider background, or more evenly from the several parts of the nation, than did Oxford, with 11 as against 3 percent having fathers in law and medicine, over 9 percent in business, and some representation of academic fathers (who were lacking in the Oxford group unless they were included with plebeians). The Oxford compilers may have grouped with plebeians some who would have been more clearly identified in the Cambridge directories;° however, totaling the last six categories to cover professional, business, and plebeian parents, we have 29 percent of the Cambridge but only 6 percent of the Oxford matriculants. Presumably those military men who sent sons to a university favored Oxford for its greater social renown. This interpretation is not gainsaid by the fact that the nobility, who hardly needed to burnish their crests, formed a larger proportion of Cambridge than of Oxford students.

Changes in the social status of fathers of university students during the century and a third were perhaps remarkable mainly for the lack of decisive trends.[7] Representation from families of churchmen held steady. Especially noteworthy was the stable position of the gentry in view of their waning position in the national population. Sons of military officers were at no time of major importance at Cambridge, though their representation there after 1830 was enlarged. Attendance of officers' sons at Oxford moved rapidly upward from 25 percent of those entering in 1762-69 to a peak of 50 percent in 1810-29 but dropped again, to 36 percent in 1870-86. No conspicuous alteration in the representation of the minor groups was revealed other than a drop in the share of plebeians at Oxford for each successive twenty year period, from 13 percent to 10 to 6 to 1 percent (in 1810-29) and less than a half of one percent thereafter. At Cambridge plebeian representation never exceeded 2 percent until 1830, after which it varied between 5 and 3 percent. In view of the changing composition of the national population, it appears that both universities became more selective as the decades passed.

Subsequent Careers of Students

Did students leaving Oxford and Cambridge universities persist in their inherited social ranks, or did they spread through the broadening vocational structure of the nation?

A first answer to this question is provided by comparing the percentages of fathers in the various status categories with the corresponding percentages for subsequent careers of the sons (using the data of Table 1). The contrasts are noteworthy. Only 6 percent of the alumni were listed as gentry in contrast to 27 percent of the fathers. This pattern was similar at both schools. Nearly three-fourths of the men became clergymen, though only a fourth of their fathers had been churchmen; this contrast was greater at Oxford than at Cambridge (the ratios of son/father percentages being 2.8 and 1.7 respectively). Rarely did Oxford sons enter military life; only 2 percent of the Oxford alumni followed military careers, though 39 percent of their fathers were officers.[8] At Cambridge there were about three-fourths as many military sons as military fathers.

At both schools law and academic life attracted many more sons than there were fathers in those categories. These gains were especially notable among the Oxford students. By contrast, the proportion of plebeian sons was somewhat less than half the share of plebeian fathers. Some upward mobility is suggested. It is evident that while law, academic life, and the higher echelons of government attracted these men, business careers held little interest for them. This lack of interest in business can be explained only on grounds of convention, hardly in terms of lack of economic opportunities.

The pattern of changes over time in the vocations of these alumni throws considerable light on the father-son contrast just summarized. At both schools, the occupation steadily preferred by a plurality of graduates was the clergy. From Oxford the church recruited between 57 and 72 percent of the students, the proportion declining slowly over the period. At Cambridge ecclesiastical alumni dropped sharply after 1830, having receded from 76 percent in 1752-69 and reaching a low of 38 percent in 1870-86.

The proportion of students who were later classified as gentry never exceeded 10 percent at either university. Next to the clergy law drew the largest cohort of students in the years after 1850; at Oxford 18 and at Cambridge 15 percent of the 1870-86 matriculants were called to the bar. Academic occupations matched the lawyers among Cambridge men after 1870. Business was never of much interest to Oxford men, though it was the career of a handful of Cambridge men after 1770, and after 1870 the percentage entering business jumped from 3 to 7. Over the period as a whole it is clear that the principal channels of social mobility for these students were the clergy (of waning importance, especially at Cambridge) and, to a lesser though growing extent, law and academic life.

Birth Order As a Selective Factor

In a society with surviving elements of primogeniture university attendance would be expected to reflect the position of a youth in his family—and the nature of this influence to be related to the social status of the family.[9]

The two universities differ in the proportion of first sons among their students; at Oxford 47 but at Cambridge only 16 percent were eldest sons. Only among sons of nobles was this contrast lacking, two-fifths of their sons being first-born at both schools. This was the lowest percentage for any stratum at Oxford and the highest for Cambridge. Apparently the factors determining whether a nobleman's son would attend a university, and which university, were unrelated to his position in his family, whereas this was not true for other students.

In each other social category first sons were less frequent at Cambridge. Oxford sons of lawyers were first sons in over three-fifths of the cases, as were about half of the students from other types of families. At Cambridge eldest sons made up 38 percent of those coming from homes of lawyers, 29 percent of military officers' sons, 22 percent of the sons of gentry, and 15 percent or less of the remaining groups. The infrequency at Cambridge of older sons from families well down the social scale suggests that younger sons were sometimes chosen for mobility with the aid of older brothers as well as fathers. The new first sons of the gentry at Cambridge suggests also that in many of these cases the elder sons attended no university since they could take up their fathers' positions while younger sons were under the obligation of finding other means of livelihood—primarily in military service and the clergy. By analogous reasoning, the relatively high proportion of first sons of lawyers at both universities may reflect the utility of such training and contacts to sons who followed their fathers' footsteps in the law.

These conclusions concerning the sons of the gentry are upheld by the proportions of first sons among students entering the various sorts of careers. As one would expect, first sons were prominent among students who were listed as "gentry". And our speculation concerning Cambridge sons of gentry fathers is supported by the small proportions of first sons among the Cambridge men entering the clergy and military life. The prominence of first sons among students who became nobles as compared with the percentages for sons of noble fathers reflects circumstances similar to those prevailing among the students who became gentry. Among the other groups the percentages of first sons are consistent with the previous data ordered by occupation of fathers. The writers infer that Oxford attendance greatly involved prestige considerations, whereas attendance at Cambridge evinced a greater admixture of other motives.

Percentage of Students Taking Degrees

The general tenor of the foregoing section is supported by the contrasting proportions of students receiving degrees from their university. Such persistence was 92 percent at Cambridge in contrast to 73 percent at Oxford, again suggesting the greater element of prestige in Oxford attendance—extending even to members of the peerage.

At Cambridge students coming from most social levels as well as those entering most of the vocational groups took degrees with fewer than 10 percent of exceptions. These exceptions were most numerous among sons of military men or those becoming officers, sons who attained high position in government, and the cases where social position was not known. Even so, the lowest percentage was 73.

The proportion of Oxford students receiving degrees averaged considerably below Cambridge and varied more from one stratum to another. Except for those of unknown origin, the percentages range between 67 (noble fathers) and 85 (medical fathers). There is an even wider scattering in relation to the students' later vocations. Thus, of the Oxford men entering military life, only 43 percent took their degrees. Of those entering business and those with no occupations given, 57 percent did so. At the other extreme, at Oxford as at Cambridge, nine-tenths of those entering the clergy, law, medicine, academic life, and "plebeian" vocations received degrees. Oxford students who were or became noblemen took degrees in only 61 percent of the cases as against 90 percent at Cambridge. There is an obvious correspondence between the requirements of definite training for a vocation and the tendency to take the degree at Oxford, while at Cambridge it was the usual practice to take one's degree.

Occupational Inheritance and Social Mobility

The core of this study lies in the evidence for status inheritance or for mobility. Table 2 portrays the status of sons classified by status of fathers for the two universities combined. Cases falling on the diagonal represent inheritance of position. In each cell, the italicized number is the ratio of the actual cases to what would be "expected" if the distribution were random. There is clearly a tendency toward inheritance of position.

All ratios on the diagonal exceed unity,[10] but they are most diverse in magnitude. Noble status is, of course, mainly inherited; this is the highest ratio (15.1). Next in order come government (13.3), medicine (8.2), law (5.3), business (4.5), plebeian (4.2), and academic (3.7). Inheritance of military status barely exceeds chance and the same is true of the gentry, a fact that is somewhat surprising unless a partial explanation be the large proportion of students from gentry families who were other than first sons. The flow of sons of military fathers into the gentry (to an extent even exceeding inheritance of military position) manifests the traditional close relationship between these two groups. Doubtless many of these sons were grandsons of gentry, though some would have attained gentry standing through military careers. Sons of clergymen entered the church to an extent only slightly exceeding chance. Occupational inheritance is strongest (apart from the peerage) in the professional, governmental, business, and plebeian ranks. For the two universities together the over-all index of inheritance is 1.29.[11]

Where else do we find combinations of father-son status to an ex-

2: OCCUPATIONAL INHERITANCE AND NOBILITY: OXFORD PLUS CAMBRIDGE, 1752–1886 (a)

ACTUAL NUMBER OF SONS AND RATIOS OF ACTUAL TO "EXPECTED" BY SONS' OCCUPATIONS (c)

Fathers' Occupations (b)	NOBILITY	GENTRY	CLERGY	MILITARY	LAW	MEDICINE	GOV'T.	BUSINESS	ACADEMIC	PLEBEIAN	NONE	ALL PROF'S. (d)
Nobility (220)	119 *15.1*	10 *1.1*	40 *.5*	14 *2.6*	3 *.2*	– *.0**	7 *2.7*	6 *1.6**	2 *.2*	– *.0**	19 *.2*	5 *.17*
Gentry (1,174)	16 *1.1*	53 *1.1*	401 *.9*	16 *.6*	83 *1.1*	2 *.1*	4 *.3*	19 *.9*	44 *.7*	5 *.5*	531 *1.0*	129 *.85*
Clergy (1,173)	8 *.4*	26 *1.1*	580 *1.3*	24 *.8*	55 *.7*	17 *.9*	8 *.9*	15 *.5*	90 *1.5*	9 *1.3*	341 *1.3*	162 *.85*
Military (1,108)	20 *.5*	83 *.5*	299 *1.3*	29 *.8*	84 *1.1*	7 *.4*	12 *.6*	5 *.4*	22 *.5*	5 *1.4*	526 *.8*	113 *1.11**
Law (110)	4 *1.0**	2 *1.8*	28 *.7*	1 *.4**	39 *1.1*	4 *2.3**	2 *1.5**	2 *.6*	12 *.4*	– *.5*	16 *1.4*	16 *.76*
Medicine (172)	4 *.6**	1 *.1**	67 *1.0*	3 *.7**	22 *1.9*	23 *8.2*	4 *1.0**	– *.8*	7 *2.1*	1 *.0**	42 *.4*	29 *2.19*
Government (27)	5 *5.0**	– *.0**	8 *.8*	2 *2.9**	4 *2.2**	– *.0**	4 *13.9**	– *.0**	– *.0**	2 *.7**	2 *.7*	4 *1.53*
Business (167)	4 *.0**	8 *.0**	69 *.8*	2 *.5**	13 *1.2*	6 *2.2**	13 *3.0**	6 *4.0**	15 *1.8*	2 *1.4**	29 *.5*	34 *1.52*
Academic (59)	– *.0**	– *.0**	25 *1.1*	2 *1.4**	2 *.5**	2 *2.2**	2 *2.9**	11 *1.8*	2 *4.0**	2 *4.0**	13 *.5*	4 *.82*
Plebeian (125)	–	–	48 *1.1*	4 *1.3**	8 *.5**	– *.0**	2 *.9**	6 *1.0**	5 *4.0**	6 *4.2**	52 *.6*	14 *.82*
None Given (1,063)	14 *.0**	42 *1.0*	479 *1.0*	34 *1.3*	50 *1.0*	25 *1.5*	6 *1.0**	31 *.9**	63 *1.0**	11 *4.2**	308 *1.2*	138 *.98*
All Prof's. (d) (1,083)	8 *.4*	3 *.9*	120 *1.2*	6 *1.3*	24 *.7*	6 *1.5*	2 *.5*	19 *1.2*	3 *1.2*	3 *.8*	71 *1.2*	113 *1.51**
Total Cases	194 *.65*	225 *.21*	2,044 *.93*	131 *.72*	363 *1.55*	86 *2.31*	64 *1.50*	94 *.34*	272 *1.33*	46 *1.50*	1,879 *.60*	71 *1.51*

(a) All figures raised by pro rata adjustment of Cambridge cases to allow for names beginning K to Z; (b) total number of cases shown in parentheses; (c) ratios are given in italics; (d) excluding fathers and sons in same professions. "Professions" include law, medicine, and academic.
* Actual and expected cases both less than 5 before raising Cambridge figures.

tent exceeding chance? First, sons of nobles distinctly preferred military or governmental (and possibly business) careers. Sons of higher government officials were unusually likely to become nobles, as would be expected. (There is a suggestion also that sons of officials were attracted to business, law, and the armed forces.) Sons of the gentry and of military men were disproportionately without a regular vocation (or at least none was known to the university), and sons of military men were over-represented among the gentry, as noted. Merchants' sons favored academic occupations and (if we may trust the few cases) medicine and official life. Sons of academic men were too few to justify generalization beyond noting a marked occupational inheritance (3.7) and some affinity for the clergy (1.1). Sons of those men called "plebeians" manifested no special preference for any non-plebeian field of endeavor.

The ties of the clergy with other groups are clarified by combining certain groups. Only three-fourths as many sons of noble, gentry, and military fathers combined entered the church as would be expected; on the other hand, only half as many clergymen as expected entered these groups. This contrast is partly due to a general movement out of gentry, peerage, and military circles and a general movement into the clergy which affects the possible range of the ratios. This is, however, a manifestation of mobility itself. Other sons (business, government, professional, and plebeian as a group) became clergymen in just chance proportions, and sons of clergymen entered this same broad stratum also to a random extent.

The church clearly functioned as a channel of mobility during this period of English history. Sons of clergymen spread into other occupations with a minimum of concentration, and men were drawn into the church from all other groups of university students in numbers not far from expectancy. This pattern points up more sharply than previous figures the central role of the clergy in social mobility at this period.

Since it might be expected that there would be an active give and take among the professions, say from law to medicine, and also between the professions as a group and other vocations, the ratios were computed so as to exclude occupational inheritance within the same profession. Sons of professional men chose another profession fifty percent more often than would be expected, which is somewhat above the over-all tendency toward vocational inheritance. (This figure appears less significant when Cambridge alone is considered.) The extent of inheritance of given individual professions is high (5.57). Except for government posts, no other occupations were entered to even a chance degree by the combined group of professional men's sons. The only instances in which men from other backgrounds favored the professions were among sons of business men (1.52) and the clergy (1.03)—ignoring the unreliable data for sons of officials.

These same relationships of inheritance and mobility are shown for the two universities separately in Tables 3 and 4. Though the general pattern is similar in essentials to that already sketched, certain differences merit emphasis. First, occupational inheritance among sons of gentry fathers is far below expectancy for Oxford—the only instance of this sort. The explanation here may lie in the numerous cases where the later occupations of gentry sons were not known. We may presume a large share of these sons to have entered the gentry stratum, which would raise this ratio too above expectancy. Second, the flow of officers' sons into the gentry is even more striking than before, especially at Cambridge. Third, the mobility among the professions for Cambridge is very little above random—it comes to 1.19; for Oxford it is 2.25 but the cases are few. The professional inheritance ratio for Cambridge was 4.46; for Oxford the cases are too few to justify citation of a ratio. Fourth, the diagonal ratios of aggregates of actual to expected cases gives an inheritance ratio of 1.43 for Oxford and 1.63 for Cambridge, as compared with 1.29 for the two combined. (Since unknowns at Oxford were mainly sons and at Cambridge fathers, the weighting in the combined table accounts for the lower ratio; the separate ratios are the more meaningful.) The difference between the over-all Oxford and Cambridge inheritance ratios are erased entirely when they are compared with the "maximum possible" inheritance for each institution. [12]

Occupational Mobility of Cambridge Students: 1937-1938

Without turning to primary sources in college archives, an analysis of the student bodies of Oxford and Cambridge in the twentieth century is impossible. No information has been found, and indeed it may be that none exists, for London or the provincial universities. There is, however, a study of Cambridge graduates in the year 1937-38 [13] to which attention will be directed shortly. As background a few remarks on developments at the two universities in the present century may be helpful.

According to a 1922 report of the Royal Commission on Oxford and Cambridge there had been a rapid increase in the number of "poor" students in residence during the first two decades of the century. The Education Act of 1902 had increased the powers of local education authorities to grant scholarships. To their actions, along with an in-

3: OCCUPATIONAL INHERITANCE AND MOBILITY: OXFORD, 1752-1886

Fathers' ACTUAL NO. OF SONS AND RATIOS OF ACTUAL TO "EXPECTED" BY SONS' OCCUPATIONS(b)

Occupations(a)	NOBILITY	GENTRY	CLERGY	MILITARY	LAW	MEDICINE	GOV'T.	BUSINESS	ACADEMIC	PLEBEIAN	NONE
Nobility (93)	56 _17.5_	2 _.6_*	15 _.5_	3 _2.7_*	1 _.3_*	— _.0_*	3 _2.7_*	—	— _.0_*	— _.0_*	13 _.3_
Gentry (722)	1 _.04_	11 _.4_	243 _1.1_	1 _.1_	22 _.7_	—	2 _.2_	—	21 _1.1_	3 _.8_*	418 _1.1_
Clergy (597)	8 _.4_	11 _.5_	246 _1.3_	9 _1.3_	13 _.5_	—	3 _.4_	—	27 _1.7_	4 _1.3_*	276 _.9_
Military (1001)	18 _.5_	70 _1.9_	270 _.8_	14 _1.2_	69 _1.6_	7 _2.0_	20 _1.7_	7 _2.6_	14 _.5_	5 _.9_	507 _1.0_
Law (15)	2 _4.0_*	—	3 _.6_	1 _5.0_*	1 _1.7_*	— _.0_*	2 _10.0_*	—	1 _2.5_*	— _.0_*	5 _.7_
Medicine (65)	2 _.9_*	1 _.4_*	23 _1.1_	1 _1.3_*	5 _1.8_	2 _10.0_*	—	—	3 _1.8_*	1 _2.5_*	27 _.8_
Plebeian (70)	— _.0_*	—	19 _.9_	— _.0_*	— _.0_*	— _.0_*	—	—	2 _1.1_*	1 _2.5_*	48 _1.4_
None Given (10)	1 _2.5_*	—	— _.0_*	1 _10.0_*	— _.0_*	— _.0_*	—	—	— _.0_*	— _.0_*	8 _1.6_
Total Cases	89	95	819	30	111	9	30	7	68	14	1,304

(a) Total number of cases shown in parentheses; (b) ratios are given in italics; * actual and expected cases both less than 5.

4: OCCUPATIONAL INHERITANCE AND MOBILITY: CAMBRIDGE, 1752-1886

Fathers' ACTUAL NO. OF SONS AND RATIOS OF ACTUAL TO "EXPECTED" BY SONS' OCCUPATIONS(b)

Occupations(a)	NOBILITY	GENTRY	CLERGY	MILITARY	LAW	MEDICINE	GOV'T.	BUSINESS	ACADEMIC	PLEBEIAN	NONE
Nobility (61)	30 _13.0_	4 _1.4_*	12 _.5_	5 _2.3_	1 _.2_	— _.0_*	2 _2.5_*	3 _1.6_	1 _.2_*	— _.0_*	3 _.2_
Gentry (215)	7 _.9_	20 _2.0_	75 _.8_	7 _.9_	29 _1.5_	1 _.2_*	1 _.4_*	9 _1.3_	11 _.7_	1 _.4_*	54 _1.2_
Clergy (274)	— _.0_	7 _.6_	159 _1.3_	7 _.9_	20 _1.5_	8 _1.1_	3 _.9_*	4 _.5_	30 _1.5_	5 _1.6_	31 _1.2_
Military (51)	1 _.5_*	6 _2.5_	14 _.6_	7 _3.9_	7 _1.5_	— _.0_*	2 _1.7_*	4 _1.1_*	1 _.4_*	— _.0_*	9 _.9_
Law (45)	1 _.6_*	1 _1_	12 _.6_	— _.0_*	18 _4.5_	2 _1.7_*	1 _.7_*	5 _1.6_	— _.0_*	— _.0_*	5 _.9_
Medicine (51)	1 _.5_*	— _.0_*	21 _1.0_	1 _.6_*	8 _1.7_	10 _7.1_	1 _1.7_*	— _.0_*	2 _1.6_	— _.0_*	7 _.5_
Government (13)	2 _4.0_*	— _.0_*	4 _.7_	1 _2.0_*	2 _1.7_*	— _.0_*	2 _10.0_*	1 _.0_*	1 _.5_*	— _.0_*	7 _.7_
Business (79)	2 _.7_*	4 _.7_	33 _.7_	1 _.4_*	6 _.8_	3 _1.4_*	3 _3.0_*	6 _2.4_	7 _1.2_	2 _2.5_	13 _.8_
Academic (28)	—	—	12 _1.0_	1 _1.0_*	1 _.4_*	1 _1.3_*	1 _2.5_*	—	5 _3.3_*	1 _1.1_*	6 _1.1_
Plebeian (27)	— _.0_*	— _.0_*	14 _1.2_	2 _2.0_*	4 _1.7_*	— _.0_*	— _.0_*	2 _2.5_	2 _6.7_*	—	2 _.4_
None Given (502)	6 _.3_	20 _.9_	228 _1.0_	16 _.9_	24 _.5_	12 _.9_	3 _.5_	15 _1.3_*	30 _1.1_*	5 _.9_	143 _1.4_
Total Cases	50	62	584	48	120	37	17	42	97	15	274

(a) Total number of cases shown in parentheses; (b) Ratios are given in italics; * Actual and expected cases both less than 5.

crease in private funds for scholarships and the improvement of local schools, the Commission attributed this alleged increase of students from less exalted homes, financially speaking. Whether the new students were poor in relation to the whole population is another question. The data on scholarship students in the two years before the first world war, cited in support of the conclusions, show that 892 scholarships and "exhibitions" were awarded at the two universities, of which 425 went to boys from the cheaper boarding schools (fees under £80) or from day schools with fees under £10. The other 467 presumably attended expensive schools. These scholarships were still regarded as honors primarily, without respect to financial need— a situation that had gradually come to prevail after the reforms of the mid-19th century. The movement to require a "means test" as well as merit for scholarship students was gaining momentum and found expression in the 1920 provision of 180 State Scholarships for all universities together. One may infer, however, that few boys from low income families were yet to be found at Oxford or Cambridge, however improved the situation compared to earlier generations.

Among the students leaving Cambridge in 1937-38, two-thirds had come from the "Public" schools and nearly one third had been holders of university scholarships (Table 5). The high prestige occupations of the present day were recruited disproportionately from those students who had attended "Public" schools. These fortunate men were less likely than their relatively impecunious fellows to enter teaching, research, or government service—the occupations heavily favored by the scholarship holders. The explanation lies both in the distribution of opportunities and in considerations of status (in addition to pre- ferences conditioned by specific family associations). The clergy occupied a middle ground. As would be anticipated, those vocations attracting a smaller proportion of ex-Public School youth received a comparatively large percentage of scholarship holders.

The differences in the occpuational categories used in the alumni register of Cambridge and in the 1937-38 survey limit comparison of the backgrounds and careers of recent students with those of an earlier period. Certain contrasts are nevertheless evident. Clergy fathers had declined from about 30 percent of the total in 1850-86 to 7 percent in 1937-38, while business fathers (even excluding busi- ness-scientific) burgeoned from around 10 to over 30 percent. In short, these two sectors of the population changed places, though clergy families are still represented more than proportionately to their numbers in the population at large. The share of students coming from military, law, and medical homes altered little over the sixty-

5: PERCENTAGES OF CAMBRIDGE STUDENTS EDUCATED AT "PUBLIC SCHOOLS" AND HOLDING SCHOLARSHIPS, 1937-38

Occupations	Number of Students (a)	Percent of Students (b)	Percent from "Public Schools" (c)	Percent Holding Scholarships (c)	Percent of Fathers (b)
Business:					
Commerce	427	17.8	76.1	21.1	32.5
Scientific	275	11.5	72.7	24.4	13.7
Government Service	234	9.8	54.3	53.8	8.3
Professions:					
Clergy	147	6.2	61.2	38.1	7.4
Military	197	8.4	85.8	7.1	7.0
Law	247	10.4	78.1	13.8	6.6
Medicine	268	11.2	82.5	16.0	8.1
Architecture	37	1.6	78.4	13.8	0.8
Teaching	364	15.2	45.3	54.1	6.9
Research	99	4.1	44.4	49.5	(d)
Miscellaneous	91	3.8	78.0	(e)	6.5
Nil	(d)	(d)	(d)	(d)	2.1
Unknown	262	(b)	60.7	(e)	(b)
Total	2,648		67.7	29.7 (e)	

(a) Occupations the students planned to enter or were entering as reported by their tutors for all students leaving the University in the years 1937 and 1938.

(b) Percents of known cases. The "unknown" students were 9.9 percent of the 2,648 cases. Among the students with occupations given there were 289 for whose fathers this information was lacking, or 12 percent of the 2,295 cases; no information was published concerning occupations of fathers of students classified under "unknown." All percentages computed from data given in the source.

(c) Percentages computed from data given in the source. They are related to the occupations of students, not to those of their fathers.

(d) No fathers were classified under "research" and no sons under "nil." Some research fathers may have been included with miscellaneous" and sons with no occupations are among the "unknown" cases.

(e) No information given for those with unknown or miscellaneous occupations. The percentage for the total excludes these cases, referring to the 2,295 students in known and specified occupations.

Source: Cambridge University, Commission on Special Inquiry into University Education as a Preparation for Business. *University Education and Business,* 1945, Cambridge University Press.

odd year interval. The recent data do not identify gentry families, who are in any event a less clear-cut social category today; we may assume them to be included under "nil" and to have become a less important source of students. Evidently the university today has become an integral part of business-class life.

The pattern of careers (or intended careers) among Cambridge students also has become quite unlike that of the third quarter of the 19th century. The proportion of alumni becoming clergymen dropped from 49 percent in 1850-69 and 38 percent in 1870-86 to a mere 6 percent in 1937-38. Military men increased slightly, law declined from a sixth to a tenth, but medicine continued the earlier increase from 4 to 7 and now (in the 1930's) 11 percent. Academic sons (teaching plus research) became slightly more numerous, 19 instead of 10 and 16 percent; perhaps some of the business-scientific group should be allocated here. The form of presentation of the modern data allows no inference about noble or gentry sons, but general knowledge entitles us to conclude that these strata are a smaller part of the much larger student body of today.

The categories of business and government are also confusing since the earlier data included as plebeians all business employees and all but the highest officials in government. We may obtain a rough composite picture of student occupations by combining business, plebeian, and government of the earlier tables to compare with government plus business (both commerce and scientific) of the later data. Taken together, these groups made up 5 percent of the 1850-69 and 10 percent of the 1870-86 matriculants (excluding "unknowns"); they were 39 percent of the known cases in the modern group. (About a tenth of the cases were "unknown" in both the earlier and the later data). Evidntly the relative importance of this combined group has increased about fourfold over the sixty years. Although Cambridge is still unrepresentative of the universities of England, the changing character of England is clearly reflected in these students, and one would be justified in underlining the conclusion that Cambridge today is an institution for business rather than for the church and the gentry.

A comparison of occupations of sons with those of their fathers reveals the effects of two influences—over-all trends in the size of different vocational groups and the role of the university itself in fostering or facilitating inter-generation shifts in occupation. In 1937-38 as in the third quarter of the nineteenth century, the number of sons entering (at least initially) both the academic and the legal professions was double the number whose fathers had been engaged in these pursuits. At the very end of the earlier period students entering medicine came to exceed by a third the number of fathers in this profession and in the 1930's the excess was about three-fifths. The moderate shift toward military careers indicated by the 1937-38 data may well have reflected the international tensions of that time. Though Cambridge was much more heavily patronized by business families in the

20th century, and a much larger proportion of students subsequently
followed business careers, the university was more a channel out of
than into business. The proportion of students entering business was
only two-thirds of the proportion coming from business homes.

It has been emphasized repeatedly that Cambridge during the 18th
and 19th centuries had served as an important recruiting agency for
the clergy; the son-father ratios had been consistently above unity.
But as the 19th century went by the ratios dropped and today the
vocation of clergy is not fully replaced among the Cambridge student
body; more sons enter the university from clergy homes than take
Holy Orders.

How frequent was occupational mobility among the modern Cambridge students? Table 6 tells the story; the ratios were derived in the
same manner as for the 1752-1886 series. [14]

A smaller degree of occupational mobility among the recent students than a century ago is perhaps the impression yielded by a cursory
inspection of Table 6 in conjunction with Table 4. The inheritance
ratios of the diagonal are 2.61 for the later and 1.63 for the earlier
series. Before putting too much weight on this conclusion, however,
the composition of the two populations of students must be taken
into account. [15] Each of the ratios on the diagonal of the 1752-1886
table except clergy, gentry, and "none given" was 2.40 or higher.
Unknown cases were omitted from the publication of the recent data
and the category of gentry was not used. If we exclude nobility,
gentry, and unknowns from the earlier table, the diagonal ratio for
the remainder is still 1.64; but if we exclude the clergy also it becomes
5.81. It was the prominence of the clergy among both fathers and
sons in the earlier sample that accounted for much of the relatively
high mobility found there. In the earlier period sons of clergymen
took up their fathers' vocation only to the extent of 1.34 times expectancy; among the recent group of students from clergy homes
occupational inheritance occurred to an extent measured by the ratio
of 4.76. This was the highest diagonal ratio in 1937-38 (excluding the
few architects). The clergy have declined in relative prominence within this student body since the mid-19th century; and, what is of
greater significance, they have lost their earlier role as a channel of
mobility and have become an inbred group. The least occupational
inheritance in the modern data is among sons of businessmen.

The interrelations among the separate professions within the recent
student body as contrasted with the earlier pattern may be seen by
comparing the "All professions" columns and rows of Tables 4 and 6.
In the earlier period the ratio of actual to expected cases for inter-

6: OCCUPATIONAL INHERITANCE AND MOBILITY: CAMBRIDGE, 1937-38

ACTUAL NUMBER OF SONS AND RATIOS OF ACTUAL TO "EXPECTED" BY SONS' OCCUPATIONS(b)

Fathers' Occupations(a)	BUSINESS COMMERCE	BUSINESS SCIENTIFIC	GOV'T.	CLERGY	MILITARY	LAW	MEDICINE	ARCH'T'RE	TEACHING	RESEARCH	ALL PROF.'s
Bus.; Commerce (651)	180 *1.5*	45 *.6*	51 *.8*	42 *1.0*	40 *.8*	89 *1.2*	60 *.8*	7 *.7*	102 *1.0*	35	258 *.98*
Bus.; Scientific (275)	63 *1.2*	101 *3.2*	12 *.5*	12 *.6*	6 *.3*	10 *.3*	18 *.5*	5 *1.1*	37 *.9*	11	70 *.62*
Government (166)	20 *.7*	16 *.8*	49 *3.0*	5 *.6*	16 *1.2*	12 *.6*	12 *.6*	2 *1.1*	28 *.9*	6	54 *.79*
Clergy (148)	11 *.4*	3 *.2*	16 *1.1*	49 *4.8*	12 *1.0*	8 *.6*	16 *.9*	1 *.8**	28 *1.1*	4	53 *.79*
Military (141)	21 *.8*	8 *.5*	15 *1.1*	2 *.2*	50 *4.1*	13 *.5*	7 *.4*	3 *.4**	21 *1.2*	1	44 *.74*
Law (132)	19 *.8*	7 *.5*	11 *1.1*	4 *.4*	9 *.8*	63 *4.0*	11 *.7*	3 *1.3**	6 *.3*	2	17 *.43*
Medicine (163)	12 *.4*	6 *.3*	7 *.4*	6 *.5*	12 *.9*	13 *.7*	92 *4.6*	– *.0**	13 *.5*	2	26 *.53*
Architecture (19)	1 *.3**	5 *2.2*	– *.0**	– *.0**	– *.0**	3 *1.3**	– *.0**	7 *23.3*	3 *1.0**	–	6 *.77*
Teaching (138)	12 *.5*	20 *1.3*	16 *1.3*	6 *.7*	7 *.7*	4 *.3*	5 *.3*	4 *2.0**	50 *2.5*	14	13 *.40*
Misc. & Nil (173)	39	31	17	8	16	15	12	3	21	11	
Unknown (289)	49	33	40	13	29	17	35	5	55	13	
Total Cases (2295)	427	275	234	147	197	247	268	37	364	99	
All Professions(c)	44 *.53*	38 *.73*	34 *.78*	16 *.51*	28 *.75*	20 *.54*	16 *.47*	4 *.59*	22 *.43*		*.48*

(a) Total number of cases shown in parentheses; (b) Ratios are given in italics. For further explanation see footnote 14. (c) Excluding fathers and sons in same professions. "Professions" include law, medicine, architecture, and teaching.

professional mobility (excluding clergy because of their preponderance in numbers) was 1.19 for Cambridge separately (1.51 for both universities), showing a better than random degree of shifting back and forth from one profession to another. But in the 1937-38 group there was instead an antipathy among these groups, with interprofessional mobility only .48 times expectancy. The inheritance within the given professions (law-law plus teaching-teaching, etc.) was 4.46 for 1937-38 compared to 3.74 in the earlier years. Despite the antipathy among the professions in the 1937-38 data, mobility between the professions in the aggregate and other occupations appears to have been slightly less than formerly. In the years 1937-38 a third of the sons of professional men moved out of the professions and two thirds of the students entering the professions came from nonprofessional homes. In 1752-1886, 58 percent of the sons of professional men left the professions and four-fifths of the professional men came from non-professional homes.

In both periods men moving out of the professions as a group appeared in all other categories in less than chance proportions—if we except the unreliable figure showing affinity with government (1.25) in the earlier data. But the pattern of movement differs in some respects. Sons of professional men in 1752-1886 revealed strong aversions to military (.45) and business (.26) pursuits, and few of them appear among the nobility and gentry. Among the 1937-38 students, by contrast, sons not following the professions of their fathers entered military service and business-scientific pursuits more readily than they shifted to other professions (including clergy). Government was the most favored choice. As in earlier years they showed an aversion to commerce, though to a less extent than formerly.

Sons in the professions in the earlier period descended in chance proportions or more from the gentry (1.01), clergy (1.12), military (1.13), business (1.07) and plebian (1.20) circles, as well as from professional homes. The 1937-38 men who chose the professions were rarely from any profession other than that of their fathers; excepting occupational inheritance, commerce and the clergy were the most strongly represented among them. The representation of business-scientific was remarkably low.

Viewing Table 6 as a whole, the recent patterns of vocational "affinities" other than those of occupational inheritance may be seen by seeking out the non-diagonal cells with the highest ratios, the disaffinities or "antipathies" by focussing on those with the lowest ratios.[16] The starred items of Table 6 have been ignored.

Affinity between parental occupations and certain filial occupations is evident as schematized below. The sons of physician and of lawyer fathers entered no particular vocations to an extent above chance.

Fathers in:	contributed sons to:
Business-Commerce	Law (1.18); Teaching (1.01)
Business-Scientific	Business-Commerce (1.24); Architecture (1.14)
Government	Military (1.16); Teaching (1.07)
Clergy	Teaching (1.19); Government (1.10)
Military	Government (1.06)
Architecture	Business-Scientific (2.17)
Teaching	Business-Scientific (1.34); Government (1.28)

Viewing these same relations from the sons' positions:

Sons in:	had fathers in:
Business-Commerce	Business-Scientific (1.24)
Business-Scientific	Architecture (2.17); Teaching (1.34)
Government	Teaching (1.28); Clergy (1.10); Military (1.06)
Military	Government (1.16)
Architecture	Business-Scientific (1.14)
Teaching	Clergy (1.19); Government 1.07); Business-Commerce (1.01)

Sons who were themselves doctors or clergymen revealed no specially favored origins; both these groups also showed an unusually high degree of inheritance.

Within this network of father-son career affiliations there are just three reciprocal relations other than occupational inheritance. These are government with teaching, government with military, and business-scientific with architecture.

Next to be considered are the antipathies, since a study of mobility involves consideration of where people do not move as well as where they do move. The lowest eleven ratios were selected (the next higher one being triplicated). All of the low architecture ratios are in starred cells and hence were omitted.

Looking first, as before, at the fathers' side of the relationship:

Sons of men in:	seldom entered:
Business-Scientific	Military (.26); Law (.31)
Clergy	Business-Scientific (.17); Business-Commerce (.39)
Military	Clergy (.20); Medicine (.40)
Law	Teaching (.28)
Medicine	Business-Commerce (.29); Business-Scientific (.31)
Teaching	Law (.26); Medicine (.32)

Or viewing these data in relation to the sons' positions:

Sons in:	seldom had fathers in:
Business-Commerce	Clergy (.39); Medicine (.39)
Business-Scientific	Clergy (.17); Medicine (.31)
Clergy	Military (.20)
Military	Business-Scientific (.26)
Law	Teaching (.26); Business-Scientific (.31)
Medicine	Teaching (.32); Military (.40)
Teaching	Law (.28)

Sons of government fathers showed no antipathies for any other vocations, and government sons had unusually diversified origins; government does not appear in this list of antipathies. Also, sons of men in business-commerce spread themselves over the whole range of occupations without markedly neglecting any category. The only reciprocated antipathy indicated is that between law and teaching.

Generalizations and interpretations of these paterns are hazardous because of the limited numbers of cases, but a few suggestions are worth noting. In general it would appear that affinities—over and above the cases of occupational inheritance—involve either (1) an upward movement in the status from the fathers' to the sons' generation (a movement to be expected on the gasis of general knowledge about the society) or (2) an illustration of particular similarity of background (as in the linkage between architecture and business-scientific). The antipathies are in part the other side of the same coin; but some of them elude ready interpretation and many of these ratios are statistically less reliable.

Highlights of Change

The comparison (shaky as it may be in details) between Cambridge University students of the years just preceding the late war with those entering college from 50 to 180 years previously unmistakably highlights several aspects of the social and economic transformation in England during the past two centuries. Cambridge remained, with Oxford, a luxury university giving scant welcome to the youth from lower-class homes, especially when we consider the pattern of student social life along with the mere money costs. The data available for this study do not permit inference as to the difficulty of entering these universities now as compared to the period before the great Reform Bill, although auxiliary information referred to suggests that the rigors of selection have been relaxed in some measure.

These modest sets of data give the definite impression of a student body altered in accord with changes in the society from which the students come and in which they take their part as they leave university halls. Where once there were sons of gentry and clergymen there are now sons of business and professional men. The principal channel of mobility is no longer ecclesiastical. In certain respects business has taken this place, though with a difference. The university in previous generations prepared men to take Holy Orders—many more students than fathers were clergymen. In 1937-38 there were not more sons than fathers in business (not even more sons than fathers in the church) among these students. Rather, successful men of business sent their sons to Cambridge (and doubtless to Oxford) to prepare for other lines of work. Business operated as a channel of mobility first outside the university, and then through the university sons of businessmen flowed into other fields. Nevertheless, it seems beyond argument that today as yesterday a father from a humble vicarage would have been more likely to have a son in the university than would a man in business.

All assessments of social mobility eventually meet the difficulty of scaling the vocations at any given time and of comparing the scales for different dates. In full awareness of this difficulty, the writers hazard the judgment that vertical mobility today via the universities studied may occur within a vocational group quite as much as between vocations differing sharply in social or economic standing. No doubt the clergy of a century ago were a transitional group, the recourse of younger sons of gentry and the avenue through which those without land might in another generation or two approximate the envied status of the gentry. To be sure the clergy were typically in modest financial circumstances and their sons benefited economically as well as socially from university attendance. Perhaps one might be justified in saying that in the older day such mobility as was fostered by the university was mainly circulation within the upper-middle and upper classes, with the clergy as the primary channel for change of status, while today it is circulation within the middle class with no occupational group uniquely forming a major bridge to other status segments of the population. The net result may well be a larger opportunity today for the more modestly placed families but not more total mobility via the university. Land ownership and high church rank were unambiguous signs of status in the simpler stratification of yesterday. Today stratification appears along more dimensions within each of the broad rubrics of the modern population.

The Education of Distinguished Men

Though Oxford and Cambridge have not typified higher education in England since the rise of competing universities, yet it would
be bootless to deny their continuing eminence. Any novel or Blue
Book will testify to their function of sustaining the status of certain
groups in the nation—at least up to World War II, and this study can
do no more than provide a background against which it may be possible
in the future to analyze post-war changes. The newer universities
cannot be compared directly with the older two in the absence of
any registers of their graduates comparable to those used here.
However, some perspective may be gained by an analysis of samples
of men listed in *Who's Who* and in the *Dictionary of National
Biography.*[17]

Who were these men deemed worthy of mention in the two volumes?
The Eminent Men (as we will designate those listed in the *Dictionary
of National Biography*) for the most part are recognized for their
accomplishments; this is the more selective of the two sources. *Who's
Who* includes many more men and incorporates peers and often sons
of peers with little accomplishment; inheritance and achievement are
here more evenly balanced. It should, therefore, occasion no surprise
that professional men are more numerous among the Eminent Men
as well as among their fathers, or that they should be more frequent
among those in *Who's Who* whose fathers' statuses are not given than
among those for whom the lists gave paternal status (Table 7).

The exalted position, socially if not politically, of the military in
English society is reflected in all the distributions. That they were
most numerous among the *Who's Who* men with identifiable fathers
and least numerous among the Eminent Men presumably reflects
the same factors that explain the opposite pattern for professional
men. Comparisons with the occupations of Oxford or Cambridge
University students and their fathers may be made readily by means
of data presented earlier. The small proportion of gentry in the list
of Eminent Men and in *Who's Who* is due in part to the fact that
this category was a residual one; outstanding men are listed under
the occupations in which they made their reputations. Many of the
noble sons appear to have become Eminent Men (when they did)
as members of Parliament or the Government; men of non-noble
origins who achieved such recognition themselves were not classified
"noble."

Over two-fifths of the men in *Who's Who* not reporting their fathers'
status (presumably in many cases because it was humble) had no

7:   PERCENTAGE DISTRIBUTION OF OCCUPATIONAL-STATUS
CLASSES: EMINENT AND *WHO'S WHO* MEN AND THEIR FATHERS

	Fathers		Eminent Men (a)	Men in *Who's Who*	
	Eminent Men (a)	*Who's Who*		Fathers Specified	Fathers Not Specified
Nobility	7	18	7	11	—
Gentry (b)	11	17	1	5	2
Clergy	14	22	4	10	11
Military	9	19	12	30	22
Government	2	3	13	8	11
Business (c)	22	3	6	8	15
Professional (d)	21	14	37	18	25
Plebian (e)	14	4	20	10	14
Total cases	180	188	180	188	166

(a)   Sample from the 1922-30 *Dictionary of National Biography*. All fathers
were specified.
(b)   The 1 percent of Eminent Men who are gentry is only one case, an eminent
book collector.
(c)   Including engineers, as in the 1752-1886 classification.
(d)   The "professions" were defined to include law, medicine, academic, and
architecture.
(e)   Eminent and *Who's Who* "plebians" include: authors, artists and musicians,
actors, social workers, trade union leaders, and plebian revolutionary politicians. "Plebian" fathers include authors, artists, and musicians, also skilled
laborers.

formal higher education (Table 8). Over a third of the *Who's Who*
men from known backgrounds were without higher education, as
against only a quarter of the Eminent Men. Sons of unknown fathers
were the most likely of the three groups to have attended universities
other than Oxford and Cambridge or the military academies. Oxford
and Cambridge were attended by a larger proportion of Eminent Men
than attended other British universities. Foreign universities (included in section C of Table 8) were of negligible importance except
among the *Who's Who* sons of unknown fathers, and this group has
little representation in the military academies. This last fact, taken
together with the appreciable percentage of *Who's Who* men of
known fathers attending military schools, testifies to the above-
mentioned strong role of the military in the English status structure.

There is a close association between the institutions at which these
men received their university education (if any) and both their own
and their fathers' social or occupational positions. Most of the sons
of nobles or the men who were nobles either attended the two famous
universities or did not receive higher education. A similar pattern ap-

pears among the gentry. The armed forces schools were prominent only among military men, many of whom were sons of military fathers.

Oxford and Cambridge stand out as sources of education for professional men and for distinguished children of professional men (including the clergy); but there is one important qualification to this generalization. Professional men listed in *Who's Who* and failing to mention their paternal occupation relied upon other universities than

8: UNIVERSITY ATTENDANCE IN RELATION TO OCCUPATIONS OF DISTINGUISHED MEN AND THEIR FATHERS

| | Percentage Distributions (a) | | | | |
| | By Fathers' Status | | By Own Status | | |
	Eminent Men	Who's Who Men	Eminent Men	Who's Who Men Specified Fathers	Who's Who Men Specified Fathers Not
		A. Oxford and Cambridge			
Nobility	61	35	92	25	°°
Gentry	42	38	°°	60	50°
Clergy	65	56	63°	77	45
Military	19	14	—	9	14
Government	°°	49°	30	50	26
Business	37	50°	10°	33	8
Professional	69	37	56	53	22
Plebian	12	—	45	36	22
All Groups	44	36	44	36	22
		B. Military Academies			
Nobility	—	12	—	5	°°
Gentry	11	9	°°	10	—°
Clergy	4	10	—°	—	—
Military	38	29	57	37	11
Government	°°	17°	13	6	—
Business	7	—°	—°	—	—
Professional	5	7	—	—	—
Plebian	4	—	—	—	—
All Groups	8	13	8	13	2
		C. Other Colleges and Universities			
Nobility	8	6	—	10	°°
Gentry	26	9	°°	—	—°
Clergy	23	19	37°	17	44
Military	12	11	5	7	13
Government	°°	17°	35	13	26
Business	28	17°	30°	7	25
Professional	13	26	28	38	63
Plebian	24	57	8	32	22
All Groups	21	16	21	16	33

	D. No College or University				
Nobility	31	47	8	60	°°
Gentry	21	44	°°	30	50°
Clergy	8	15	—°	6	11
Military	31	46	38	47	62
Government	°°	17°	22	31	48
Business	28	33°	60°	60	67
Professional	13	30	16	9	15
Plebian	60	43	47	32	56
All Groups	27	35	27	35	43

(a) Those attending institutions in more than one of the groupings were listed where they last attended as undergraduates. The four percentages for each status (one in each column of each section of the table) add up vertically to 100.

°° Less than 5 cases in all educational categories together.

° From 5 to 10 cases in all educational categories together.

Oxford or Cambridge. These other universities have clearly played a greater role in facilitating mobility among men coming from families that have "not yet arrived."

The most diversified educational backgrounds appear to characterize those attaining fame in government service and the *Who's Who* men in "plebeian" occupations. In view of English traditions a larger representation from Oxford and Cambridge among those entering government service (especially in the earlier period of the Eminent Men) would not have been surprising. Eminent Men who were following "plebeian" pursuits were for the most part educated at Oxford or Cambridge or nowhere; but the later *Who's Who* "plebeians" attended the other universities in about the same proportions as they went to Oxford and Cambridge.

How does it happen that a considerable proportion of famous "plebeians" in all three groups attended Oxford and Cambridge? This is in part a reflection of the peculiarity of the category "plebian." The arts and letters are among the occupations classified "plebian." These are occupations in which relatively few men are engaged, but those few are disproportionately likely to attain fame. Plebian fathers were sometimes skilled workmen, but the famous "plebian" sons were something else. Some were trade union leaders and leftist politicians; more were authors and artists of one kind or another. A cabinet maker's son may succeed in becoming a famous man, but it is unlikely that he will have an opportunity to attend the sister universities. An eminent writer himself classified as "plebian" may, on the other hand, come from a wealthy family. Indeed, of the renowned plebians of all three groups who were educated at Oxford and Cambridge four-fifths were authors and only one (not an author) was from a "plebian" home.

A much more definite clue to the role of the universities in fostering the rise to prominence from humble origins is to be found in the figures on the percentages of famous sons of plebians attending those universities. There were no sons of plebeian fathers in the Who's Who group who attended Oxford or Cambridge; the majority of these men went to other universities and the remainder had no higher education. Among the Eminent Men the figures are less striking, but despite the earlier period to which they refer the pattern is the same. Moreover, the evidence of the case histories shows that the few Eminent Men from "plebeian" homes who attended Oxford or Cambridge were not really of humble circumstances to start with. Although Oxford and Cambridge turned out far more than their share of great men, they did not reach deep into the social pyramid. The data clearly justify the efforts of those who strove to found and nourish the newer universities.

APPENDIX

The 1752-1886 students of Oxford and Cambridge analyzed in this study are a sample taken from the *Alumni Oxoniensis* and the *Alumni Cantabrigiensis*, which are listings of those who matriculated at the two universities. The second and later series of each of the sets of volumes were used. Oxford's lists included the years 1715 through 1886 and those of Cambridge 1752 through 1900; the overlapping years 1752-1886 were therefore selected for study.

The names in each set of volumes are arranged in alphabetical order, Oxford's volumes being complete and those of Cambridge running through the letter J. (The compilation was halted during World War II and has only recently been resumed.) A total of 1,632 pages in the Oxford volume was estimated to contain 65,280 names, since there are approximately forty biographies per page. The available Cambridge volumes contain 1,741 pages with approximately 20 names on each page; when completed they will probably consist of about 73,900 names if the proportion of students with names beginning with K to Z is the same as that of Oxford. Thus for Oxford the Universe consists of 100 percent of the names as compared with 48 percent for Cambridge. Every twentieth name in each volume was taken for the samples, excluding those with honorary degrees only and those who were deemed "privilegiatus" as in the case of barbers, cooks, and similar servants at Oxford; in such cases the twenty-first name was taken, but counting for the next case was based on the previous name.

The most serious problem involved in comparing and combining the two series is that the systems of classification of status or occupation differ. The categories at Oxford are mainly class rankings rather than occupational rankings, and they confuse the issue by including also new occupational rankings in the later years. Cambridge gives specific occupations for the most part, such as banker, ship-builder, druggist, admiral — with the exception of nobility and esquire or gentry fathers and sons. The following classification was developed as the most workable compromise to be used for both universities.

1. Nobility
2. Gentry (including county officials, esquires, and non-noble members of Parliament when this was the only information given)
3. Clergy (including the range from clerk to bishop)
4. Military (army and navy)
5. Law (including the range from solicitor to judges in the Queen's Chancery and the Inns of Court)
6. Medicine (including dentists)
7. Government (Colonial and Domestic Administration and Diplomats)
8. Business (including merchants, bankers, brokers, manufacturers, and engineers—the entrepreneurial and management men)
9. Academic (including teachers at all levels, educational administration, antiquarians, researchers, etc.)
10. Plebians (including "plebian" unspecified, business employees, government employees other than those in the preceding categories, yeomanry, husbandmen, writers and journalists, musicians, painters, etc.)

The defects of this classification are obvious. Since it is a mixture of status and occupational categories, a few of those listed as nobility and gentry may have been engaged in other occupations and vice versa. More important, the category of plebeians at Oxford is broader than in the Cambridge classifications, especially for the first half of the period under review. The Oxford list includes in this group some business and professional men who would have been grouped in other classifications at Cambridge.

The reliability of a sample is always suspect if the proportion of "unknowns" is large. "Not given" cases of Oxford fathers were few (10 in 2,676), but for a full third of the Cambridge fathers status was unknown. The careers of 50 percent of Oxford and 20 percent of Cambridge students were not on record. In assessing the implications of these unknowns for the conclusions of the study we must rely upon internal cross checking and upon a priori reasoning.

It seems reasonable to assume that few fathers or sons from the peerage were among the unknowns. This does not preclude non-noble sons of nobles, or non-noble fathers of enobled or collaterally inheriting noble sons occasionally being unknown to university alumni records, but such cases would hardly have proportionate representation among the unknown sons.

As for the other groups, comparisons of the various tabulations point to a distribution of cases that is not markedly biased. In the least reliable data (the supplementary Oxford series for the sixteenth and seventeenth centuries) it was apparent that the percentage distribution of fathers' ranks for 1612-21 when one seventh of the cases were unknown was not unlike that for 1572-1611 when there were few unknowns.

Next, the reader may notice that although the percentage of unknown Cambridge fathers is high, yet the percentage of Cambridge fathers who are of lower status is greater than at Oxford, for which nearly all fathers' ranks or occupations are given. At Cambridge also there is no tendency from one twenty year period to another for a lower percentage of unknowns to go with a higher proportion of lower class fathers. So far, then, we are not impelled to conclude that the "unknown" are heavily weighted with men of lesser status.

The much smaller proportion of military fathers in the Cambridge group might suggest that many of the unknown Cambridge fathers were military. However, on a priori grounds this seems most unlikely, for the War Office lists of officers would have been available to the compilers of the Register. Also the Eminent Men and *Who's Who* men of military fathers who attended one of the two sister universities chose Oxford with few exceptions.

The ratios of plebeian sons to plebeian fathers are the same at both universities despite many more unknown sons at Oxford. The ratio for the military at Oxford is exceedingly low, but here again the availability of War Office records suggests that a disproportionate number of military sons among the unknown Oxford sons is unlikely. The data on distinguished men corroborates this conclusion in part, for distinguished military men were less frequently from Oxford and Cambridge than any other group except the business *Who's Who* sons for whom fathers' occupations were not listed. With respect to sons' occupations, just as for fathers', one observes no association from period to period between percentages unknown and percentages in lower status categories.

In analyzing the two-way tables relating fathers' and sons' occupations, it was observed that the ratios to expectancy among the "not givens" approximated randomness, though the findings were ambiguous. The sons of unknown fathers were distributed broadly among the vocations; likewise, students with unstated occupations appear to have come from varied backgrounds, though with somewhat higher selectivity than those becoming clergymen. From the percentages of students taking degrees one negative conclusion appears reasonable; this percentage is low for students of unknown vocation and for those whose fathers' status is not given. In line with the text discussion of these data it is inferred that the professions may have been under-represented among the "not stated" sons.

Who then were the "not stated" sons? We have suggested reasons for believing that the military were not over-represented among them and may indeed have been under-represented. Probably the professions and certainly the nobility were under-represented. On a priori grounds we might expect business and plebeian fathers and sons to be over-represented though the internal evidence of the data suggest that these were not a major source of "unknowns." For the most likely upward bias among unknown sons, we must turn to the gentry. Sons of gentry origin are recorded as having no occupation more frequently than is expected, and the inheritance ratios for the gentry are surprisingly low—especially at Oxford where the proportion of "unknown" sons was so high. The "not given" sons were disproportionately not first sons. On the assumption that younger sons from the gentry are uncommonly likely to be men of leisure there may have been an over-representation of such men in the category of unstated occupations rather than too few. The lesser gentry sons would be less easily identified some time later than some of the other groups, although the gentry status of fathers was no doubt indicated in the records of Oxford students at the time of matriculation.

The internal evidence that plebeians are not disproportionately represented among the unknown fathers and sons is given some support from the *Who's Who* data—especially the case of *Who's Who* men with plebeian fathers. None of these men attended either Oxford or Cambridge. On the other hand, *Who's Who* sons of gentry generally attended the sister schools if they had university training at all, and these institutions are well represented among the *Who's Who* sons of clergy. Finally, among the 1937-38 Cambridge students it is of interest that the percentage who attended "Public Schools" is not especially low among the students whose parental status was unknown.

In conclusion, unknown cases appear to have approximated a

random distribution among the fathers of Cambridge students. The only evidence of a likely over-representation among the unknown sons is for Oxford gentry sons; if this bias in fact occurred the extent of overall occupational inheritance at Oxford is slightly understated and that for inheritance among the gentry themselves may be grossly understated. Concurring in advance with the judgment of those readers who regard the results of the present study as definitely tentative, the authors would nevertheless affirm that the data appear to lack gross systematic bias.

REFERENCES

1. *The Older Universities of England: Oxford and Cambridge*, by Albert Mansbridge, Longmans, Green, & Co., New York, 1923, p. 107.

2. *Op. cit.* p. 108. (The secession of the English church took place in 1534.) In his *Oxford and Cambridge Matriculations* J. A. Venn shows that there was a sharp drop in attendance when there were no longer monks and friars in residence but that within two decades the increased enrollment of gentry brought the totals above their former level.

3. "Register of the University of Oxford" by Andrew Clark in *Oxford Historical Society Papers* V. II, Part II, 1887, p. xi.

4. Mansbridge, *op. cit.*, p. 117; the next quotation is from p. 111 and the one after that from p. 118.

5. Due to the deficiencies of the published census statistics for this period, one cannot relate the number of fathers to that of men in various callings. General knowledge, of course, tells us that professional men, the peerage, and the wealthy were a minute proportion of the total population. In respect to the low representation of academic men, one infers that clergymen-teachers, who were many, were classified in the registers as clergy.

6. See the appendix on this point.

7. These data for separate twenty year periods have not been printed due to space limitations.

8. It is quite possible that many of the Oxford sons with occupations "unknown" were military, but even making full allowance for this leaves a decline indicated. See the discussion of the "not given" cases in the appendix.

9. The tabulations on birth-order and degrees are omitted; these or other detailed tabulations can be made available upon request.

10. With one exception—for families where the information on status of both father and son was lacking; this is not true for the two schools separately, a point to which we shall return.

11. The sum of actual cases in diagonal cells divided by the sum of "expected" cases in those cells.

12. Diagonal random expectancies were computed assuming the number of sons in each occupation to be the same as the number of fathers for the total student population. The sum of these expectancies was then divided into the total number of cases, giving the "maximum possible" ratio for Oxford of 3.50 and for Cambridge of 4.64. The extent of inheritance observed and possible as

a maximum are then found by subtracting 1 from the appropriate inheritance ratios. When the resulting observed figures are divided by the maxima, we get an inheritance of .17 times the maximum possible in each school. For the combined table the same ratio is only .06.

13. *University Education and Business,* by the Cambridge University Commission on Special Inquiry into University Education as a Preparation for Business, 1945, Cambridge University Press.

14. Unfortunately we cannot determine the occupations of students in the miscellaneous or unknown categories, and "research" was not distinguished among fathers as it was among sons. Hence the table is based on cases for which occupations of both generations were stated and excluding "research" sons. To include the omitted cases would bias the results toward smaller occupational inheritance since the sons of fathers in miscellaneous, none, and unknown categories would necessarily have appeared in other cells. The bias is not great; the ratio for the diagonal drops from 2.61 to 2.58.

15. A comparison of observed with "maximum possible" inheritance does not eliminate the contrast. In the recent data observed inheritance was 32 percent of the maximum possible whereas it was only 17 percent for Cambridge in the period 1752-1886.

16. The index of inheritance (diagonal ratio) is the ratio of all actual cases in diagonal cells to the total expected cases for those cells; i.e., 2.61. The ratio of non-inheritance, conversely, is the total cases in all other cells divided by the sum of expected cases in these other cells, or .74. Thus any ratio in a non-diagonal cell of .75 or higher indicates an "affinity" between the particular fathers' and the particular sons' occupations. By the same token, "disaffinities" are shown by ratios below .74. The text discussion considers only the highest 12 pairs of father-son occupations in which the ratios exceed 1.00 and the lowest 11 pairs with ratios of .40 or less.

17. Only natives of Britain were included. Each third male case was taken from the 1922-30 volume of the *Dictionary of National Biography.* The men deceased in this decade might have entered college during 1850-90, a group (herein called Eminent Men)) roughly comparable to the matriculants of the last four decades of the 1752-1886 period. The *Who's Who* men (the first male name on every tenth page of the 1940 issue) might have been in the university around 1900. The occupations for both samples were classified as in the main study.